Get Your Ex Back

Helpful Tips To Getting Your Ex Back

By: Jason Scotts

TABLE OF CONTENTS

PUBLISHERS NOTES

DEDICATION

This book is dedicated to those who still have hope to getting back their ex.

Introduction

There are literally thousands of couples across the world who have broken up with their perfect partners (for them) due to very simple misunderstandings. It's sad to think that many of these break-ups could have been completely avoided if each person just had a clearer understanding of what their partner was thinking and what they wanted from the relationship.

Unfortunately, because men and women are biologically so different to each other, there are specific things we each do that can easily drive a partner away rather than keeping them close, as we'd intended. Of course you may be hurting. You might even be completely bewildered as to why your relationship has ended at all. But the reality is that good relationships break up all the time … needlessly.

That's right — needlessly. If men and women had a little more awareness of how the opposite sex was thinking, then break ups need never happen. In fact, you could have turned your relationship with your ex into a life-long happy partnership where neither of you would ever consider looking further afield.

If you've recently broken up with the love of your life, don't feel that all is lost. There's still hope that you can win your ex back and it's actually easier than you think. Even if you've tried everything you can think of to let your ex know how much you want to be together, perhaps you have noticed, it's not working out the way you'd planned.

The problem is that we're not taught about how the opposite sex thinks, so it's mostly a mystery to most people. We're stuck trying out tactics that we think may work without ever considering what our partner would prefer instead.

This book will explain some very simple tactics that can give your ex a completely different view of the person you are and get him or her to fall in love with you all over again.

Are you ready to bring your ex back into your life again? Are you really ready for them to fall in love with you, deeper and stronger than the first time around?

Then let's get into the good stuff...

Chapter 1- When Good Relationships Turn Bad

It's unfortunate that sometimes even the very best relationships go sour, but, even if we cannot see it, at first, there is always a reason.

There are actually countless reasons why good relationships turn bad and end up with a break-up. You might have endured meaningless arguments or you might have simply found that your ex stopped communicating with you completely and then pulled away, leaving you in the dark about what was happening.

People who are hurting and unsure of where their partner is at in the relationship often end up doing the exact opposite of the things they should be doing to bring their ex back to them.

This is because men will tend to do the things that seem logical to a man and women will tend to try the tactics that they would want to see. It is a big lesson to learn that men and women think differently. Applying male logic to the problem of winning back a female is usually counterproductive as is the reverse i.e. applying female logic to the process of winning back a male.

The really sad part about this is that, despite their best intentions, in these situations, both men and women tend to do things that will actually turn off and push away the person they really want to bring back into their lives and without even knowing they're doing it.

This means they're often doing the complete opposite of what they should be doing to bring back their ex and make that person a part of their lives again, yet they're totally unaware of it. Think about it. Is what you're doing right now to get your ex back working for you? Or is it just driving that person further away from you, making you feel even worse than you already do?

Let's look at some of the things men and women think about during relationships and how they view the actions of their partner. These insights can often bring about a much deeper understanding of what might have gone wrong within the relationship and bring a deeper knowledge of what to do when good relationships go wrong.

CHAPTER 2- MEN AND WOMEN ARE BIOLOGICALLY DIFFERENT

You may think that this is stating the obvious, but apart from the obvious differences, there are vital hormonal and other biological differences that set us apart.

For example, did you know that in order for men to decrease their stress levels, they'll often look for ways to increase testosterone? This means they'll watch the news when they get home from a long day, seeking to find ways to spark their own "fix it" mode. This means they may enjoy grappling with other people's problems because it sparks a need within them to try and solve the problems of the world. That may be what he is thinking about even though he might be stationary on the sofa. He will be unavailable for real-world problems while he is getting his own stress levels sorted out.

When their testosterone levels are raised, they'll feel much better about the world and seek to remedy their own problems only after they've calmed down enough after a hard day at work, where they've spent the day trying to show their loved ones how much of a good provider they can be.

Unfortunately, women have the completely opposite biologically drives, which can cause problems within a relationship. For example, when a woman has increased testosterone levels within her body, it can actually increase her stress levels, causing her to want to fight about trivial matters that her partner can't possibly understand.

In order to reduce stress levels, women will find ways to generate the hormone oxytocin. Curiously, oxytocin is known in non-scientific circles as the "cuddle hormone" and it's been linked strongly to maternal behavior as well as being the bonding hormone that makes a woman want to bond more strongly with a partner.

Now, for women to create oxytocin, they need to feel loved, cherished and appreciated. When they tend to feel as though their partner is withdrawing from them, for any reason, this actually causes the hormone testosterone to flood their system instead which raises their stress levels and can tend to make them defensive.

For a man to experience a decrease of testosterone, conversely, he experiences a similar reaction where his own stress levels increase and this makes him defensive too.

Interesting stuff ... eh?

Chapter 3- How Hormones Can Ruin A Great Relationship

Think about how many times you've been in a great mood, looking forward to seeing your partner. You would have spent the day doing things that made you feel better about yourself. If you're female, you might have spent some time working through your stress by talking to your girlfriends about various issues you have, which would have raised your oxytocin levels.

You would have been feeling great!

Yet, when your ex finished work for the day, he would have been stressed and wound up after a hard day. He has absolutely no desire to talk about his problems because this increases the wrong type of hormone within his system. All he wants to do is unwind – maybe solve the problems of the world sitting in front of the TV for a little while.

But he's now faced with a partner who wants to talk and share and cuddle and be loving right at that moment where his stress levels are high and perhaps even unmanageable. He hasn't had a chance to unwind from his own stressful day yet, but he's now confronted with a partner who's feeling fine and doesn't seem to understand his needs at all. This is a simple example but do you see the problem here? Even the best relationships can be destroyed by these simple hormonal differences between men and women if there's a lack of understanding about them.

Of course, there are relationships that go wrong for other reasons.

Chapter 4- When Relationships Go Wrong For Other Reasons

What happens when you've done everything right and your ex still pulls away from you?

There are times when relationships go wrong for no reason that you can figure out at all. You may have thought everything was going great, and yet your ex decided to stop calling you, stop returning your messages and pull away from the relationship completely as though you weren't there at all.

The shunned partner often feels as though they've done nothing wrong, yet the partner who has withdrawn completely may have completely different ideas about where the relationship was going in the first place.

The truth is, when humans fall in love, they release a particular hormone that is very similar to the one released by people suffering from Obsessive Compulsive Disorder (OCD). This is one reason why people in love can't think of anything else but the person they're with, can't eat, can't sleep properly and can't concentrate at work.

Of course, just because you're feeling this way doesn't necessarily mean your partner was feeling the same thing at the same time as you were. Just as not everyone gets hungry at the same time, not everyone gets the same feelings at the same time.

The unfortunate part about this is that sometimes one person within the relationship will begin to think about progressing the relationship further. They'll spend time thinking about the future and playing out various scenarios within their minds about what will happen once the partnership progresses past the dating stage.

This can lead that person into believing that the relationship has actually evolved into something much deeper than has really happened, whilst the other person may simply be still trying to figure out what's going on with their feelings. This is sometimes called the 'instant relationship'. One partner thinks they're just dating whilst the other one is already in full relationship mode and wondering why their partner doesn't appear to be reciprocating.

The biggest mistake anyone can make in this situation is to try to convince their partner that they should be together or convince them about how much they love them. When men see this behavior in women, it can be enough to make them want to slow things down or even break away, wondering what is going on. They view their partner as somehow needy and desperate and they can sometimes pull away or even withdraw completely. Desperation and insecurity in a woman is a total turn-off for men.

Yet, there are plenty of men who are guilty of doing the exactly same thing to the women they adore. They may try to convince her that no one loves her as much as he does and try to reason with her that he's better for her than another man. The problem with these scenarios is that they have no real grasp on what they're doing wrong.

CHAPTER 5- THINK BACK TO THE BEGINNING TO FIND THE ANSWER

In almost every break-up, the solution to getting your ex back lies in thinking right back to the very beginning of the relationship.

What was your partner like when you first met? More importantly, what were you like when you were together at the beginning?

Chances are you were both on your best behavior. You both worked hard to be sure the other person was having a good time. You also both would have overlooked any minor quirks in personality or behavior, simply because you were driven to make a good impression on the other person. Now think about the last time you spent time with your ex. Were you both enjoying each other's company? Or were you fighting, stressed, upset or worried about what the other person was thinking?

If you were not getting along very well, the chances are that the image your ex has of you in his/her mind is the image of you arguing, angry, crying, upset and worried about the future of the relationship. This isn't conducive to thinking happy thoughts about a positive, happy future together. Instead, they are probably thinking about ways to find someone who is more like the person that you actually were when they first met you.

That's right – the person you were when you met. He/she would have fallen in love with the happy, confident, positive, motivated, independent person you were when you first met. You would have made him/her feel happy when he/she was with you and they would have enjoyed wondering when you were free in your busy schedule to see them again.

So ... what changed?

CHAPTER 6- MISTAKES YOU MIGHT HAVE MADE

Are you guilty of trying to convince your ex to get back together with you, even after they've broken up with you? Sure, your heart might be breaking and your intuition is telling you that this is the person you were supposed to spend the rest of your life with. But does your ex feel the same way?

If you've tried calling your ex, texting, emailing or sending messages, trying to convince them that you're the right person for them, chances are you're driving them even further away. The problem with these constant attempts at contact is that your ex is seeing them as an act of desperation on your part. Nobody, male or female, likes desperation. It reeks of insecurity and clinginess and that's a really unattractive trait in anyone.

Both men and women find confidence very attractive in the opposite sex. A confident person, who knows what they want and doesn't need another person to make it happen for them, is ultimately very appealing to everyone.

Yet a person who suddenly becomes very sure that the only way they can be happy is by attaching themselves to you is all of a sudden very unattractive. Remember that your partner probably fell in love with a happy, bubbly, confident version of you.

The miserable, lonely, desperate version of you isn't quite the same thing and your ex might be wondering what happened to the person they fell in love with. After all, the unhappy person in front of them right now isn't making them feel the same feelings they felt when they were falling in love.

Would you feel like you were spending time with a great person if you only heard misery, arguing, begging, pleading and attempts at convincing, every time you were anywhere near that person? Of course not; you'd want to leave and go to spend time with people who are a bit more fun wouldn't you?

So what do you do if you've already fallen victim to the trap of pleading or even begging them to come back to you and, as a consequence, it's driven your ex even further away? Well that's what we'll consider next because, even if you're guilty of sending constant messages or calling your ex or texting, emailing or messaging them, it may not be too late to salvage your broken relationship.

CHAPTER 7- REVERSING PAST PROBLEMS

No matter how badly you want to, your first step in getting your ex to come back to you is to avoid contacting your ex in any way. Stop texting. Stop calling. Stop emailing. Don't ask his/her friends about them - just stop.

Now, think back to who you were before you met. You were probably getting along just fine with your own life. You would have had your own job, your own friends, your own interests. Go back and get them rolling again the way they were before you met your ex.

Even though you might not feel like it and your own sad emotional state might make you feel like sitting at home waiting for the phone to ring … don't. Put a smile on your face and spend time with your family and friends. Hang out with people who make you feel good about yourself and your time with them.

Avoid any negative friends or people who will let you become morose about your lost love. These people won't help you get your ex back at all so ensure you stay away from them. The key here is to bring back that happy, independent version of yourself that your ex fell in love with in the first place.

After a little while, your ex will begin to wonder why you haven't called or contacted them in any way and they'll begin to worry about you. You are not there yet, when this happens, but you will have made a good start. Think about it: for your ex to worry implies that there must still be a level of care for you.

So – big lesson here - stop contacting them and instead, work on what's happening within yourself.

CHAPTER 8- BREAKING THE FAIRY-TALE IMAGE OF RELATIONSHIPS

Hollywood movies are largely to blame for the fairy-tale images most people have in their minds of how love works. Somehow, the silver screen has managed to make us think that after a lot of drama, conflict and arguing, the love of our lives will suddenly come to their senses and we'll all live happily ever after.

This isn't realistic and it's something that tends to happen in idealistic romance movies rather than in real life.

The truth is: your ex is not the key to your happiness.

You are.

You don't need to have another person in your life to be happy or fulfilled. You only need yourself and your own interests, hobbies, passions and things that ultimately make you feel good.

When you first met your ex, chances are you were already happy, independent and confident. These are extremely attractive qualities to the opposite sex. So go out. Have some fun. Hang out with friends. Watch silly comedy movies that don't make you think about him/her or that upset you. Buy a new outfit. Get a new haircut. Work out a bit. Spend time making yourself look and feel good.

When you look good, you feel good and when you feel good, you become attractive to everyone around you again. Your confidence levels will naturally come back up and you'll soon find things to be happy all around you.

There is another reason for this tactic.

Not only will it help you move past the fact that you've broken up with your ex, but it will help you get back in touch with the person you used to be when your ex first met you and fell in love with you.

Chapter 9- Re-Establishing Contact With Your Ex

When you've spent a bit of time raising your confidence levels back to where they were before you met your ex, you'll begin feeling better about yourself. You'll also be in a much better position to meet with your ex once again.

Sometimes, once you stop contacting him/her, it's enough to make them want to pick up the phone and call you to make sure you're okay. If they have done this, you know he/she still cares for you in some way, but don't make the mistake of meeting too soon. You want to be sure you're feeling more like your old happy self before you do this.

However, if he/she hasn't called and you've spent a couple of weeks working on your own self-esteem, you might want to try a friendly phone call just to say 'hi'. Don't insist you want to talk about the relationship and don't invite him/her out for a coffee. Just let them know you wanted to say 'hi'. This also gives you an opportunity to begin a conversation about what you've been up to in recent weeks since you split up. Let them know you've been going out, having fun and doing things for yourself.

It's also okay to 'let it slip' that you've been thinking about him/her sometimes, too, but don't let the initial conversation get much more involved about the relationship or the break-up. This is very important.

Also very important: before you end the conversation, mention that it would be nice to catch up at some point.

But don't suggest a time or a place.

Chapter 10- Playing Hard To Get, Not Hard To Want

It's no secret that men love to chase what they think they can't have. Unfortunately, many women take this too far and decide to date someone new in order to make their ex jealous. This never works. By immediately jumping to another guy, you'll be letting him know that your relationship wasn't important to you and you've moved on already. Even if he still did have feelings for you, he's not likely to act on them.

The idea of playing hard to get is simply remembering not to drop everything you're doing and rush to him/her the moment they call. Let the call go to voice mail and call them back when you're in a happy frame of mind.

If they suggest a date, you can agree to it, but make sure you change the proposed day. For example, he/she might want to meet for coffee on a Friday. Agree to meet for coffee, but tell him/her that you're busy Friday and that Saturday would be better for you.

It makes no difference what else you're doing on the day suggested – call a friend, watch a movie, wash your dog – whatever. Just be sure he/she understands that you're busy with your own life. If they want to be a part of it again, then they will need to work a little to gain your attention.

When you do eventually meet up with them again, pre-arrange another meeting so it forces you to be on a time limit. Explain that you can't stay long and that you need to leave at an exact time. This will probably mean cutting your conversation short and, if you've been enjoying each other's company, it will definitely leave him/her wanting more.

Once you've gotten through your first meeting together, don't be tempted to call them right away to arrange another date. Leave it a few days and see if they call you first.

Remember, he/she has still got images in their mind of the reasons you broke up. One meeting with you being your old self isn't going to be enough for them to forget about the problems that split you up. You will need to spend time rekindling those feelings for you if you really want them back.

Be careful with your tactics in playing hard to get, though. You really don't want to become one of those people who is hard to want. These are the folks who cross the line of confidence, over into arrogance. They have strong opinions and they're willing to voice them, even if it means causing arguments. They're stubborn about being completely blameless in the relationship's break up and they blame their ex for doing everything wrong.

If you find your thoughts crossing into negative territory when you're with your ex, be prepared to leave the date and get out while the going is still good. If you don't, you risk losing him/her for good.

CHAPTER 11- REKLINDING YOUR EX'S LOVE FOR YOU AGAIN

Think about it: your ex got together with you because he felt a level of attraction for you when you met. The more time you spent together, the more his feelings would have grown. Then something went wrong and the relationship ended. They may tell you they don't feel the same way anymore, or they may have simply vanished into the distance, refusing to call you or answer your messages.

Even though the fire might be out, you can guarantee there will still be embers glowing in the back of their mind somewhere. It's your job to fan those embers back into a spark and ignite the flames once again. If you're serious about winning your ex back, you'll eventually need to get to a point of discussing what went wrong in the relationship and why it ended. Just be sure you don't make the mistake of doing this too soon.

After an emotional break up, you both need time to sort through your thoughts and work through what might have happened. Of course, when you do meet up with your ex again after being apart for a while, it's important that you don't bring up the subject of the break-up during that first meeting. Simply allow them to see the happy, confident version of you that they fell in love with right back at the beginning.

You may find that some people will be curious to know why you didn't try to get them to come back or demand to know why they left, or do any of the things they would do in that situation. This curiosity alone can often be enough to make them pick up the phone and ask for another date, just to see what you'll do next.

Of course, there are other people who will decide that you must be playing some kind of mind game and they'll continue to remain distant from you. If your ex is one of the latter, leave it a week after you've met and then call them to arrange another date to meet up on a friendly level.

While these tactics might sound very simple, they're designed to get your ex thinking about you when you're not around. The more they think of you when you're apart, the higher the chance they'll want to call you again.

CHAPTER 12- REBUILDING A STRONGER RELATIONSHIP

Wishing for the old relationship you once had to be brought back together is futile. After all, the relationship you had is ended. It didn't work. You don't want to fix a broken relationship. Instead, you want to work on building a new version of the relationship, only this time on a much stronger foundation.

Think about some of the things you really enjoyed about your past relationship before you broke up. Now consider some of the parts you know could cause problems or made you unhappy. Really be selective about which parts you want to carry forward into the new relationship with your ex and which bits you want to leave behind.

When your connection with your ex has been re-established and you're beginning to date on a regular basis again, it's time to discuss what might have gone wrong in the previous relationship. If your ex is unwilling to talk, let it drop until they are ready to discuss it. After all, if you're playing 'hard to get' the right way, they should begin looking for ways to get your attention, so they'll soon find the right time to talk about what went wrong.

However, rather than ask what went wrong, try asking what they would prefer to see done right, instead. This gives them a valid opportunity to put their problem solving skills to work and try to find ways to develop a stronger bond between you. Focusing on the positive aspects of what you both want to enjoy in a relationship can be a happy way of dealing with a sensitive issue and turning it into a bit of fun between the two of you.

If you decide instead to focus on the problems of the past or the negative aspects of the break up, you could find that it turns your conversations back to negative territory. You risk starting an argument this way. Stick to looking for the good things you can both do instead.

When you both have a clearer understanding of how you want your new relationship to be, it's much easier to rebuild it on a solid foundation.

CHAPTER 13- TOO FAST, TOO SOON

Many people instantly assume that once you're dating your ex again, it must mean you're back together in a relationship. However, your partner may not think this way. Dating is simply spending some time with each other, going out, doing things you enjoy, but it's not a relationship. Not yet.

Don't fall into the trap of assuming what they are thinking or feeling unless they specifically tell you. This also means you shouldn't demand to know when they think you'll be able to get back together, or you'll be heading right back towards looking like that desperate person they already pulled away from. Instead, continue having fun together. Go out on dates. Make sure you're both enjoying yourselves. And through it all, be sure you're not the one who's dropping everything the moment they call or wants to go out.

Even though getting your ex back might be your primary goal, you need to make your own personal life a main priority as well. After all, your friends, family, work, hobbies and interests are what make you who you are when you're not with your ex. They're an important part of you and they help you to keep your confidence levels up and your stress levels down.

Every now and then, you let them know you're not available for a date and that you have other plans. You want them to continue chasing you until you're certain that their feelings for you are growing. It won't take very long before they are the one asking you if the relationship is back together or not.

Chapter 14- Earning Your Happily Ever After Badge

If you've managed to get your ex to come back to you, be sure you're not hiding who you truly are. People can learn little tricks about getting people fall for them so that they will act a certain way or say certain things to keep the interest alive. The problem with acting this way is that you're not being yourself. If you're not being yourself, then who is your partner really falling for? And what will he/she think of the real you the moment you stop the acting and start being yourself again?

If you're serious about rebuilding a relationship with your ex, don't be tempted to try tricks or mind-games or silly tactics designed to make people love you. Just be yourself. You remember – the confident, playful, fun-loving person that he/she likes.

Be the best version of yourself that you can be. Stay positive, look for the good in things, and find ways to bring happiness into your life. Enjoy your friends, have fun with your hobbies or interests.

Look your best and feel your best and your confidence will show to the world.

When all is said and done, your ex fell in love with the person you were when you first met. The chances are good that he/she will still love you for who you are. So give him/her the best version of you to fall in love with all over again.

And good luck!

ABOUT THE AUTHOR

Jason Scotts has many interests and has written many books about them. In his books, he talks about each passion how it starts, the process and how you can use it in real life situations.

Throughout the course of his career he has become familiar with the challenges that many people have and has also found quite a number of solutions to not only solve those problems but to keep them from resurfacing in the future.

As he is aware that persons do not really have the time to be deciphering text he writes in a way that is easy for everyone to understand.

Through his text Jason helps the reader to learn new techniques or to perfect old ones. He is focused on educating and informing as the main goal to help those who are seeking answers.

www.ingramcontent.com/pod-product-compliance
Lightning Source LLC
Chambersburg PA
CBHW070105260726
48658CB00002B/999